I Knew It Would Come To This

T. Anders Carson

I Knew It Would Come To This

T. Anders Carson

Spout Hill Press

First U.S. Edition
April 2013
Copyright ©2013 by T. Anders Carson

For information about permission to reproduce selections
from this book, contact Spout Hill Press at
spouthillpress@aol.com

www.spouthillpress.com
Walnut, California

Cover design by Ann Brantingham

ISBN 13: 978-0615794488
ISBN 10: 0615794483

To Daniel and Emilia

Foreword

Anyone who meets T. Anders Carson is immediately struck by his joy. Being with him, being near him is a constant reminder that life is and can always be good.

That joy infuses his poetry as you will read in this collection, but there is more than just that here. Anders's interior life is complex just as is anyone's, but his reviews (which are universally positive) focus too much on that joy because his personality is such a force.

Anders has lived much and seen much and in many ways suffered too much, more than a person should. He has dealt with molestation, the collapse of much of his family, and discord. He explores all of this pain, and the joys of a family, children, travel, and friends in this collection, which I have come to admire so much.

Anders gives us access to joy when we meet him, but here he gives us access to the whole range of human emotion, everything that someone might feel in a life, and he is an artist who feels deeply. The fact that he has gone through so much but is still so happy gives us insight on his strength, courage, and love. His poetry is a gift that will constantly inspire and change you.

I am so proud to call him my friend.

--John Brantingham, author of *Mann of War*

Contents

Landing at Iqaluit airport

Aboard the flight there are many people
on only one fifth
of the aircraft.
The rest is for cargo.
The longer the flight progresses
it gets noticeably cooler.

It is a sunny day and
the contrast of the yellow airport
and white snow is striking.
Many of the houses are
a rainbow of colors.
No earth tone policy here.
The wind is -27 C and that is cold.
Possibly the coldest wind
I've ever felt.
Next to me sat a French refrigerant installer.
He had two little ones
and is gone for a month.

I miss the kids and my wife
but this is an adventure
checked in and will unpack.

Purple knife

Bought in a market in Greece
many years ago,
it has opened countless meals
with its serrated edge.
From scrumptious cheeses
to crisp bread
lumps of butter
the occasional grapefruit
and today for the first time
it opened the sealed package
to the North.
It was a little bit
like Christmas.
Not remembering what had been put
into the two containers.

That purple knife cut into the duct tape
and revealed a slice of Southern life.
A few rolls of toilet paper
some gum
a big batch of soups to warm
the most frightened soul
and at the very bottom
two crushed boxes of cereal.

I walked down to Arctic Ventures
picked up a pint of milk for $5.59
and will enjoy the cereal
as a reminder of family gatherings
both in the morning
and late at night.

Yelling in the corridor

Last night it was an alarm
that went off just before the sleepy drizzle.
We all ignored it.
We would sleep right through the flames.
This game
a door is slammed
a child screams
and the low Innuktitut voice
begging
and the pleading to be let in.
Domestics are the same everywhere.
Voices raise
a line is crossed
and the bruises, beatings
and continual silence.
I sit on Council
in my community,
we don't have a problem.
That's why we didn't want the shelter.
Bogus on that.
It happens in all walks of life.
You hear the yelling in the corridor
and you want to hide and hide and hide
to get out of that misdirected
and inevitable
thrashing.

An Inuk at the back door

I walked over to the post office
and saw a big husky
with an even bigger chain…
They told me last week they had
a muskox pulled out and
drying in this cold.

They've come equipped from
centuries on the land.
The faces are full of stories
some blizzard sadness
others carved madness
and then a ring and he comes
to the back door to receive
the parcels.
The smile is drawn so beautifully
across his dimpled face
that I too give my wide beard grin.

This is the North,
steps made of steel
up to the back door.
God help you if you're
in a wheelchair…

To the library

At almost every branch around the world
there is that special
zone that feels right.
It can be perched in a corner
with a New Yorker in Cleveland.
It can be a 4 week old copy of Newsweek
at the American library in Nairobi.
It can be the tales of Georgia O'Keefe's place
in the Taos children's section
or it can overlook the frozen Frobisher Bay.

So close beyond the glass
that when melted you will surely hear lapping water.
Instead you see an arc of nowhere
and everywhere
that stretches in vast whiteness
that hurts my Southern pupils
and makes them shrink away
as if folding light for another season.

It comes this brightness.
It illuminates the mind
while the persistent wind
howls
a raven roams
and circles, circles, circles
looking for a safe place
to land.

Walking home

I had on -100 C boots.
My feet were warm for the first time
in winter.
It took an Arctic adventure
to realize that.
I hear a voice across the wind.

No one talks when tromping through wind or snow.
Only the chatter of small children
and the puck hitting a solid frozen board.
This was a distinct sound
and then it cleared
a window wound open
and someone hollered;

You have a really nice ass.

I haven't chuckled like that in years.
Imagine you had to reach 42
walking around on an ice cube
to get cat called.
I'm glad my L.L. Bean coat
is holding up.
I still got some moxie left
even when dressed
with layered threads
from foot to chin.

She came off the land

I haven't been here for a month.
She looked at me
with lost teeth
and a hope for some check
or scrap
or salutation.

But no,
it is a wrinkled paper
with a photocopied ID
looking and looking
through the wintry looking glass
to find some solace
before returning to that
frozen land.

In comes Lars

A Swede wanders in Iqaluit.
We do get around;
slipping into my mother's tongue
as easily as some fully worn
pair of slippers.
It is the North.
A place people go to find themselves
to try to find things in themselves
or to find things
they can buy
to be displayed.

It is as holy as ghats in India
the pyramids in Cairo
and the crooked, jarred hills
of West Virginia.

You go looking and looking
and find folks like Lars
staring you in the face.

The mirror held so clear
that the glare aches and aches
and then turns bold and bright.
Open the lines
and destroy the hatch
Papa is coming home…

Parkas and slowness

There was a group
gathered last night;
about eight of them.
Inuit with disabilities.
They had their handlers
for this opening celebration
of welcoming back the sun.
Toonik Tyme.

They clapped when the music
warranted clapping
and listened oh so close
when the singers did dancing songs
with their voices.

This pushes back the dark
and it emulates the sounds
of what is just outside.
A rolling brook
of wind across the tundra.

It is haunting yet reveals
that almost tribal healing
that comes from two
being as one.

Watching all of this
with their Canada Goose parkas.
I'm glad the slow ones
aren't pushed alone
onto an ice floe.

Skyping from the Arctic

You hear the voices of
your loved ones
and can ever hear the yo-yo
that is being manipulated
up and down.

It is far away
their physical love
but this is magic
this box
that allows the voices
of home ventures
to twirl and play
in this lonely
big room.

Working the counter

I've been at post offices before
but this one in Iqaluit
takes the marbles.
Lots of parcels.
Shopping Channel heaven
and online bliss.
A couple of calls or clicks
and it's shipped northward.

It sits in the back
with an idolatrous number in black
jotted on its spine and waits
for the seal skinned mitts
or purse
to produce the correct ID
and then release it
to the whiteness
that is just beyond
that door.

Carrying a child

It is on their backs
that the slightly bouncing women
carry their children.
The fur covers them,
a little cap with a string
to keep those little heads warm.
They bounce and move slowly
mimicking a long trek
as the children close their eyes
and wander off to sleep.
The warmth of mom
so close.

This is a family community.
One where they try to look
out for each other.
They still know the names
of their neighbors.
They've made it through another
dark, dark winter.
Sun is back
and will melt it all.

That rhythmic bouncing
moves the North
as the comfort and trust
from a child
is poignantly melded.

It is dripping

For the first time,
I see small drops of water
wick away from the icicles.
That means it is coming.
It is as if you're ten
and you put your ear
to the two iron lines
and listen for the train.

It is coming
a time for rutting,
arctic she-fox biting at potential suitors
and finding the right one,
submitting just long enough
before baring those teeth again.
It's a dangerous game,
circling one another
around and around
until you have the right one
just so.

It is coming
the time when you can wrap
your arms around your children
and swim in the lake.

It is coming
a time to be alone
taking the strained vow of silence
and looking at the wall
that sometimes moves
just a little bit closer.

It is coming

drip, drip, drip
and a ripple of hope
falls down
and covers all.

It is coming
through the tunneled darkness
into that strained;
generous light.

On the land

With a borrowed parka
and helmet
goggles and sunglasses for the glare,
I jumped onto my snowmobile
and followed the two travelers
out on the land.
The ice was so high
at times you would be
in deep a gulley with cold
all around you.
It was like Hoth in Star Wars
and driving those machines
was the closest I'll come
to flying on a land speeder.

We came to their summer home.
A cut of isolation
that wasn't frightening.
My ears rang from the stillness.
In summer
hawks sail overhead.
It is now ice and we've pulled
a whole bunch of wood.
It is gathered from work sites
or used shipping crates
as the whole community
is above the tree line.
J. asked me to sign his guest book.
I did and wrote a little poem.
It wasn't until on the return journey
that I saw something different.

Two snowmobiles came towards us.
We gathered and stopped.

They are hunters.
The word makes every bunny
pin back their ears.
They were white hunters
with guns over their shoulders
and Canada Goose jackets
to keep them warm
but he had left
his face exposed.
He had severe frost bite
giving new meaning to the words
white man.
We exchanged words and they set off.

That one beats his wife
and terrorizes his kids.
He's a hockey coach.

I wonder if that man
has taken the Respect in Sport course
that all coaches need to.
He could learn a thing or two
or not
and just go out into
that snow blindness;
not to return.

A father and two Inuit children

Racing down a hill
sleigh full of pink squeals.
This is the day with sun
and the wind
having evaporated.

Giggling of those children
beats back the hollow calling
of the Arctic raven.

Walking to work at 6:00 am

Not many in Iqaluit are up.
They are smart enough
to sleep in a wee bit.
It is siesta time when it's cold.

My beard becomes as jagged
as a cracked windshield.
My boots clump along.
Thankful for the small stones
to give some grip on the ice.
Dogs haven't even been let out
and if they're in their homes
they let this Tartan cloaked stranger
come in and out of their defensive zones.

No eye contact,
just plundering along
waiting to get into the CIBC bank
as the warmth is always there
for those who want
to take out money.

You're a liar

I want mail from my box. He hisses.

We can't do that
it is against the law. I urge

You have to have keys
to get into that small
haven where checks and bills reside.
He has no teeth
and an unkempt wavering
as the voice rises
and blasts *You're a liar!*

I can't help him.
This is the sadness of seeing
things in the post office.
Mail chutes just wide enough
to slip in a scream.
Cages of mail manually sorted.
Boxes upon boxes of lingerie,
framed prints, pillows, clothes, diapers,
tinned food and a whack of cheese.

It is Iqaluit on top of the world.
You can shake it but the global village
is not going to go down.
Long live the fly-in community.
It makes you dare to try
seeing things loudly and then fatuously
again he booms;

You're a liar!

Sweat

After being away from your wife
for two weeks
and returning to that conjugal
bed,
you think about it.
You've been trudging around the cold
delivering mail, boxes
smiles
and then that urge
that Spring urge.
It went so fast
and in such a hunger
of wanting to delve into one
that the sweat when finished
was refreshing
and more than ever
welcomed.
You're home.

Make-up

When I was 10 years old
there was a neighbor
who wanted to play doctor.
I wasn't into that then.
Then she wanted me to put
make-up on me and I wasn't
really into that either.
Imagine the amount of grit
in my beard if I wore it today.

Now,
when my wife puts on a little
of that black mascara
and touch of blue
around the eyes,
my right leg starts to shake
like a happy dog
whose had his itch scratched.
Let's dance together again
on the kitchen floor.

Folding origami cranes in an airport

You sit in an airplane
heading West
and meet a man who is close
to your father's age.

A few words are spoken
and then through courageous revealing
you hear the suffering,
alcoholism in families
choice of having the elderly stay at home
or move them into a long term care facility.

He's an administrator with a heart.
The beans are nubile and need to be counted.
There is a paradigm shift
that is taking place.
The mortgage, credit card
false security of ballooning mutual funds
persistent phone calls at home and work
asking about late payments.
asking soon becomes vagrant demands
because without that fix of minimum payment
it all collapses.
This banking pyramid that is finite.
It can only go so far.

We talk,
crawl through vistas of insecurity
and stumble upon the art of origami.
The precision generates relief.

After a snowy landing,
we head to the nearest bench
and begin to fold that crane.

Art of renewing a faith in simplicity
of community
of basking in the crazed myopia
of the future.

With one little pull
on that crafted tail,
the wings of belief
gently and determinedly
begin to move.

Early morning Los Angeles

No birds but last night
the rain came.
On TV there was a storm watch
but to my eyes it was a little
spattering of rain.

Last night,
I helped students with themes
of their essays.
Many of them writing about
my latest book.
It is odd speaking to students
when the pain is so close.

One asked
what happened to your brother
and I told him honestly
that I had made the cut.
I couldn't send any more money
for his veins.
With a family and the two younger kids
we all have those warmed stones
to walk down.

His face was kind.
He had peachy LA glasses
that lit up the room.

Now it is early morning.
Jet lag has sunk in
and I blink my eyes
in anticipation.

Reading at Mt. SAC

It was a quiet audience.
Really quiet.
For a moment I thought I was in Ottawa.
You don't know if they are really listening.
You throw in an ass poem
and they laugh
and then you *know* they are listening.

It is nerve wracking fielding the questions.
You don't know what they will ask.
You don't know what you will respond.
You just get up and lay it out.
The vile humor
paleness of getting by
and the virility of being a dad.

I just don't know how it will work out
being a writer,
a poet,
reading dreams and dreads
of how it could be.

Shooting star over Los Angeles

I woke up this morning
and got ready for a walk
through the streets.
Archie, all gray whiskered
and still trim
wanted to go for that power stroll.
Palm trees,
lush flowers
growling dogs behind gated houses.
One man had parked his car
on the lawn.
At least he made it home.

I then came to a house
full of weeds
un-trimmed hedges
and a sign on the window
to mark another foreclosure.
Even the outside light fixtures
had been removed.
The Venetian blind
hung slanted
only covering half
of the apparent loss.
While a row of unfed flowers
bloomed, briskly
under a shooting star
in Los Angeles.

Clock tower at Mt. SAC

I always look up at the clock tower
to see what time it is.
Today there was a young man
with his feet dangling over the edge.
Some thought he was going to jump.
911 was called
and then sirens,
by the time the police got there
he was gone.
He wasn't going to jump
but the call of concern
and understanding was there
behind those hands
moving the day.

Dragon of New Orleans

A sleeping dog yawns.
A cat steps over a thin puddle.
The homeless sleep in the streets.
A shade of Southern pain
is thrown over many a plantation.
It raids the kitchen after dark.
It buys non-prescription sleeping pills.
It subscribes to an awfully jealous God.
It forgets to lock the door.
It parks on the sidewalk.
It buries the dead above ground.
It bribes State Troopers
when caught speeding.
It owns 2 handguns and a shotgun.
It pays its electricity bill.
It watches nighttime comedies.
It believes the Nielsen ratings.
It has two children that are
honor students.
It is a patron of the Tree Fund
for a greener America.
It owns 2 cars.
It has visited the holy shrine of Disney.
It has slept in hostels in DC.
It believes the President.
It watches the Oscars.
It prays in close quarters.
It pops food into the microwave.
It has never been a card carrying member
of the Communist party.
It has never been mentally ill.
It will never get a passport.
It stays on Interstates.
It relies on gas prices

to reflect happiness.
It visits the sacred graves
of Arlington.
It is denied access to the Pentagon.
It rarely goes to the theatre.

For it is an aging America that rules
and with each industrial step,
with each problematic divorce,
with each gun downed child,
she grows…
Relying on hatred,
drive-by rage and
surrounded by centuries
of misplaced pain.
There she sits rocking on a porch
in Asheville,
smoking a cigar in Biloxi,
begging for a dime in New Orleans.
She stops at rest areas
and cleans up after the pets.
She stands in line,
waiting for that forgotten America.
Waiting for change…

Sometime failure

Here I am,
a man lost in neuroses
of paranoia and fear.
With each humdrum step,
I thirst for sanity
in the face of death.
I reel in the sugarcane,
spitting out fire;
chewing in the street.

I crouch in broken down Bedfords
hoping to smoothly reach
the forgotten destination.
I cry to the night goddess,
praying for a safe passage of dreams;
nightmares less frequent.
Combed and mirrored fright
left entombed
in some small but sacred
site by the Nile.

Restless mountain

Curled up,
on Mt. Sinai,
I remember the craft
of issuing false prophets
and dreams.

Suckled by insanity,
I quote the forgotten passage
that lies beneath
a desert moon.
It shines and
reveals clarity;
within a crawling realization,
the importance
of scented hookah bowls
and camel sweat,
grinds Arabic tunes
into Middle Eastern memory.
Charred teeth smile
and ask, ' *Where you go?* '
You're not sure.

The mountain
craved a personality.
It was left barren
by false prophets,
unburned incense
and the festering restlessness
that comes
with orphaned adults,
in the middle
of a shaky
Dahab sobriety kick.

A grave under a Southern tree

With a willow for a smile
and a stubborn filling station frown,
Mississippi mayhem tosses its
over-turned grapes.
Churches on either side
of God's breath
salute the main thoroughfares.

Cold hospitality,
as troopers enforce
the urinary codes
of treason.
Drive thru schemes.
Bagels by the dozen.
Grits on the side.
Would you like some hot sauce
with that?

Not caring for the fixings,
vegetables are cures
for an understated mania.
The dial turns,
lights flash,
old hazard man at the wheel.
With a dented beer can
between his legs,
he can travel
across the city
blindfolded.

The freeway to the sky is littered
with overripe drunks.
It's a shame that the road is filled
with mangled tricycles.
I told you he needs new glasses.

With a neon spin
and a dryer's capacity,
the future of America
lies beneath a clouded,
troubled pond.

Pear figures in bloom

Biting into a fresh
swig of pear flavored drink,
I remember the times
by the beach in Frösakull, Sweden.
My father had inherited
some money from a rich banker
in Cleveland.
He bought a summer home for his
Swedish wife.

Every summer we returned
and I would see
streaming down her softened face,
a reality that left her
once we came to the village.
It would flow from the dimness
of unknown phone calls
and those voices would return.

I remember the hushed cries
when we would sit on the beach;
red flag waving its drowning warning
and the polite barking
of fresh ice-cream.
The drops would drip
on the ground
making a granular fold
and then would tirelessly
be erased
by tomorrow's unforgiving rain.

Heroin

The folds
of my tears
are held in check.
I sit through
a glorified version
of drug use.
The crowd laughs
it's distinct snicker.
They seem to have left
humanity at the door.

For some,
the screen of blurry vision
starts,
when you step
on the street.
Not a day goes by
when I can't fall flat
in the face of prejudice.
Thank the gods of lottery.
When I see the path
of the struggling warrior,
needle in arm, leg or thigh,
I see the silent serpent of hatred seethe
in their eyes.
I cry in shame
for having an age
and strength of reason.
Halfway-house nightmares
shelter our unwanted
and left.

There is something
in ancient Greece

that we can silently
learn to live with.
Hemlock
laced in a garlic bow,
tied neatly around our wrists
as a reminder
of just how few steps
it takes,
to that dilapidated
curb.

Hot water

In Wales,
when we lived there in the 1990s
you had to put 10 pence in a slot
to heat up water in
the communal bathroom.
One time I placed my coins,
put on a ratty bathrobe
and went down
to a locked door.
Someone stole the warm water.
Grrrrr.

Late that night,
when my lover and I were at it
we heard another couple
downstairs.
They too were in the height of passion.
That turned the crank
for both of us that night
and we soon forgot
about the 10 pence
and the lost bath.

Stillness of Lato

Wind caresses visitors.
Wells dug in haste.
View beyond spectacular.

On Crete,
an isolated mountain,
these folk humbly
went about their business
building stone structures
and mini-theatres.
Chimes quell the northern gusts.
Olives mingle their wisdom
to all who care to listen.

In a comatose state of elation

I had for a minute a vision of lust.
It came in a strained corner of my lower lip.
It held itself up to be seen.
You can't ignore these kinds of signs.
They are there to lead us down
these damp caverns of the unknown.
They are there as markers to a distinct death.

Did I mention death?
I did.
I do hate to mention that word.
It used to trouble me so much in my youth.
That and its various forms.
Instead I have taken solace in the release
that some deaths give.
Woman battling breast cancer,
her will to live striking every stroke of uneasiness
inside of her.
Doctors once again lie about pain.
How can they do that in those firm white suits?
How can they?
Because they are well paid.
For they placate the desire to look fully
into the stoniness of icy deaths,
to have the defeated breath of facing your execution.

No, you can see some of the suffering is futile.
It doesn't need to be so charged.
It isn't as if sailing ships and
empty bottles of water in the desert
leave interminable ebullient lines of sadness.
It is far deeper than that.
It comes out in the most benign lines of an obituary.
It is left only yesterday's milk to survive.

This is the death that I speak of with some conviction.
It takes a son by surprise.
It creates a plethora of flowers and sympathies.
This is the ship of madness that one sails.
It is followed by the many fools that seem convinced
that darkness can at once be illuminated and clouded.
Instead it is but a rare beast
that offers its internal nails.
They chew on coffee
as if it was some kind of Egyptian dessert.

I parry this kind of reasoning.
It is vulgar to think that death can be silenced.
It comes in a broken grasp of angular breathing.
It sends silent messages of disaster up your right arm.
It vomits food needed for sustenance.
Creations haplessly held back
as the broken wing of a cured angel
seeps its resistance.
It dances and twirls in a ceremonial rhythm
and when the believer is hypnotized by this spectacle;
heart stops
a blood clot fills brain
and silence of muted frustration
fills the sitting room.
They have left,
gone to live and bask in the glories
of the netherworld.

Rod of insanity

The colors of death
gloat in windmills.
Strung across back ponds,
toads move from lily pad
to lily pad.
They fold frenzy in two
seeking a desire
for ritual release.

Scolding the fowl,
it flaps its frequency
and deafens the young.

The finder on the front
of the boat
measures 300 ft.
I'll take my tested
scuba tube.
Fill the tanks full
of earthly sin.
Dive
and plunge
to that forgotten depth.

A fisherman will hook
my flipper 10 years hence
and will roll over deathly
in his boat when that rod
pulls twice.
It will signal a belch of fear
that sits like a serpent
in a room.

Close those eyes
and spiral upward
through the gloom.

Death

At the school yard
the swings go back and forth.
Sometimes higher;
sometimes barely moving at all.

The swing moves higher and higher,
in a frenetic frenzy
as she reaches the epoch.

She can see the graveyard
down the street
and the swing
becomes terminally still.

The crooked fern

Besieged by enemies
of past revulsion,
strangled clouds of fear
circle looming, tainted
small towns.

In aging communities,
the crazed elders
smoke felled tobacco by the tin.
They curse the volatile youth
and serve reminders as
slyly as cooked pudding
on Easter Sunday.
Dying on that cross
plus a shotgun to the head.
It makes the strongest
want to leave the celebratory table.

It is the swaying silence
of understanding
that models structures
as fondly as those
in muted meditation.

It's true,
those snowplows
always manage
to hook a fern.

They've left the light on

It's a Thursday night
outside of the city.
Wind is in air.
Wood is in the stove.
Phone is silent.
Baby is silent.
Cat is silent.
The past is silent.
I can feel a shape of leniency
creeping across the paint.
Colors have changed.
Pellets leaving the smoldering hamper.
Bag for goodwill in the trunk.

Waiting for the call.
Waiting in a monster neuroses
that swells like fertile pigs
with stubborn rectitude.
Shaving false staccato lies
from cropped and useless tales.
A firm selling hard-on
often unlocks when least
encouraged.

Until the vaginal climate
circumnavigates south,
it will secrete nothing but a fresh
and odor-full scent.
Quick to burn.
Lingering in unwashed clothes
but for a few days.
Casual as a shooting star.
That silent phone, *phone*.
It sits unmoving.

Far less subtle
than freshly transmitted pictures.
One can almost read
the obits by the pool.
Unless a frail deer
stumbles across an autumn road,
it will never understand
spraying poisons atop fruit trees
by the lake.

A shell of flaking skin peels away.
Each fall the water breathes
an underwater breath.
Cleansing
and each winter night
as you search through the past,
you realize
that they've left the light on.

Moldy spider's thread

Listening to garbage trucks
and aggravated Tunisians,
I recall the fate of farewells
in Spring.
When blooming clouds
of leathered luxury form,
engraved streams rattle
oil lamps at night.
They fondle prayers
and hold seances under
warped bridges.

With muttering curiosity,
bottles in brown bags
pass among wart-filled hands.
Singing victory songs
and laments of old blues,
ghostly storytellers steal
dreams and visions from
the drunken listener.
Noble quests of surged sacrilege
gives stale bread that slight
green haze.
Sleeping in a hovel
divided by three sheets,
boarders must urinate in public.

Plastic springboards of decency
are left in dusty shops
as erect nipples converge
in lava showers.
Curled toes conceal silent orgasms.
Beads of sweat line the palms
of poets.

Vagrancy and unusual handcuffs
are visited in solemn, sequestered
memories.
A leather thong guides
decent scents.
A leather whip makes buttocks
blush.
A leather collar muffles
a caged whimper.

Collapsing at the foot
of regression,
our beloved spider
spins sacred webs of release.
Ecstasy locked
in bottles of pain.

Fire

There it was in the dark, dark night.
A red flame up in the air;
lights spinning around and around.
You lower the window
and an officer says

The road is closed.
It's bad.

You've spent the whole afternoon
at the local fair.
Children with ride-all-day bracelets
twirling on Tilt-a-Whirls
and sliding down slides on a potato sack.

The fire brought the family
to its knees.
Everyone got out
and afterwards it was told
that the fire had started
on the stove.
Mom had fallen asleep in the chair.
Too many night shifts
to find money for food.
Now it is gone.
Burned to the ground.
Another fire,
another loss.

Ladybug crawling up the pane

I see your little wings;
they open and close.
It is November and you are still alive,
out here in this cabin of the forest.

You see the stain of winter coming.
Birds gathering in the air
and on the lake.
Time for that flap of freedom
and the parting gift of knowing
that tomorrow will come.
Summer and all its wonderful sunshine
will return.
It is jazz that plays for your wings.
They are folding in the spaces of belief.
You just crawl and crawl.

I too search for that secret crevice.
That justified safe place
that only the fearful and pleasant can cope with;
a place beyond resonance and pure beauty.
I know that it does get easier.
Those wings open and close,
open and close
until they get heavy
and stop that gentle movement.

Blue shopping cart

It is sitting in an overgrown
gas station.
Fenced high.
Boards rotting on the building.
Pumps gone now
only stray grass
pushing out.
And there a lonely
weather-eaten shopping cart.
Blue.
Like Picasso's period.
Those tires don't spin.
You don't move produce any more.

Now just modern waste
behind the fenced curtain
waiting for those underneath tanks
to stop leaking.

Crawling the mast

I hurt when it bites me.
That movement of the old,
scaring the sometimes new.
I can see the forceful cut.
Fresh forgotten tears.
A jumbo rainstorm of inertia.
It comes to us,
in double transfers to the toilet.
Four arms lifting us to that
pity potty.
Soiling our way to the moon.
With hackneyed dentures;
a cradle of sad wants
inside the walls of the bizarre.

I can see the fence posts
lined outside.
They are well-staked
and completely swell
in a painful jubilance.
I knew this would come along
with picking pink dresses for coffins
and making mourning sandwiches on the side.
It comes in a balloon
filled with overweight helium.
Barely lifting off the ground.
A bellboy's hand pleading
but no sweaty tip.
It comes through the bullet clouds.
It falls on the fragrant shadow
of suffered sobriety.

It stumbles around singing
lover's tunes in a 1968 leather jump suit.
Ah to lose weight as the King could
and he found it all in a can...

A lamp of certainty

When a neighbor fools around mentally
with your wife,
it's hard to forgive.
But if you don't,
it'll fester like some Civil War wound
open,
abscessed
ready to fall off.

I'm forgiving this loss of sanity
but for an instant.
Playing with the young
as if they were a bug in a glass cup.
I arrive in Florida
and his breath of resistance follows.
He calls at night saying he might come.
I purchase lottery tickets
to console my uneasiness.
Hoping it will buy some freedom.
I think of the lake
and it's surrounding islands.
Chainsaws fill the air.

A snowmobile crashes through the ice.
Damp clothes become heavy.
A kick of life slowly ceases.
Anger hungers for release.
It has helped me pass through many detours
in my short and crippled life.
I understand.

Upon my return home,
light of neighbor signaling hope,
that not all signs have gone out.

Frenzied height

Curving rapidly
up the mountains of incest,
the paths and cobblestones
entwine to collect the lust
of all creatures.
Dogs in heat
cradle the insanity
of laying in old islands.
Clutching a grasp of light,
contentment seethes
in relaying truth
on this side of reality.
Crushing the folds of steps,
dust lingers
in ancient cracks.
Sitting underneath
the crest of our military,
flashing bullets slaughter
restless foreigners
itching for a fight.
Rebels cross themselves readily
as if asking for a plainer
form of justice.

Under the roll of Cerebus' sight,
the lingering scent
of battered faces,
slaughtered heads
and blood dripping
from a leather boot,
marks the passage
towards
the frequent howl
of a crippled man.

Depression

An Argentinean friend of mine
had a mother who was depressed.
When he would leave her
to go to work in the morning,
she would sit in the library with a book
and he knew that when he returned
nine hours later
that she would still be sitting there,
reading from the same
unturned page.

At the edge of darkness

Standing outside;
it can follow destruction.
I can smell the coffee
slightly burning in the pot.
It reeks its rancid pickings
into a jumble of rapid heartbeats
and spirals.
I can taste the failure
that comes with living
beyond your dreams.
I can truly see hatred
in each smashed glass of
anti-nazi bookstores.
I can fake the smiles required
when distant relatives die
and are subtly burned.
It is seen after each gavel stroke
at an auction.
The articles,
everything you've ever lived or played with as a child,
sold to the hungry and weak
to be caressed or crushed.

I can see the drool falling
down grandma's lips;
her codeine stare.
One eye wandering.
I can see the framed prints
of Picasso's erotic works.
Legs and pubis.
Breasts and fragile earlobes.
Teeth beckoning to leave
slightly reddened marks.
I can see in the darkness

of a quarter moon.
I can watch the subtle scrapes of a cat
prowling the yard for mice and meals.
I can taste the essence of summer
with each bite from the BBQ.
I can sit and visit with the stars.
Clones of a distant sadness;
light a beacon for help.

I can feel the back of a strap.
It is hard and long and cuts
producing tears and isolation.
I can see the puddle of semen
in my belly-button.
It always gets caught when I masturbate
for I am an inny.
I can taste the fragrance
of oiling my lover's flesh.
A wind teases our protected hairs.
Sensation pulsing.

I can scream a thousand un-arrested screams
when releasing into her womb.
Cry of wanted and unwanted children.
Sun teases the reflected moon.
A sunset always leaves a lingering
and stifling aftertaste.

Hometown

It is closed on Sundays,
except the liquor store
they've opened that too.
For those tempted there's an out.
I walk down the street
to the lake.
There is a park there now
for all to share.
Even a gazebo and music
in the summer.

It is evening and the mosquitoes
have started their little buzz.
It's time to run behind the screens.
It's our national bird.
My hometown is home
with all the blemishes
chipped paint
and permanently rusted
parked cars.

Mystic doubt

Carriages of children
are raised
for the world to see.
They drool and dribble
their unnatural senses
as quietly as a man
condemned to die.
Even a mother's docile hand
can't save them.
Her canal is but a passage
of doubt.
It hangs,
in the center of sanity,
like a hung slab of beef.

Rotting flies
surround the presence
holding the vicious thoughts
of revenge at bay.
The cry of children
is heard in the distance.
It supersedes
the drum of thunder.
Rattle in frail fist,
they torment parents
who can only control
their rage by slowly
masturbating in the tub.
Through the locked door
they hiss the words…
I'm busy.

We are all frail
little orphans
fit for the county zoo.
I confess that sometimes
the paying crowd can become
quite monotonous.
So in a semi-crowd pleasing sweep,
I scratch the hair under my arms
and swing wildly
from that rotting tire.

I knew it would come to this

Battlefields of strained sorrow
sit beneath the shade of torn oaks.
I can see the man with a blind eye.
I can coax the past but with one blink.
I pray to the shrine of sacrilege.
I know that these are condemned buildings
but I need to rest
and I am tired of the street.
10 trips to the detox.
I thought it was only 3 or 4.
10.
It is a perfect score in diving.
It is a number I equate with the living.
Huddled in walls of sobriety
your veins want numbness.
They search the day for silence.

In this silence,
one copes with thoughts of desperation.
Walls as thin as paper origami birds.
Stains as full as felt on a new sofa.
It is beyond walls that some sense of reality begins.
It is beyond the wall which is within.
I know,
I have seen darkness
and it sometimes shades out hope.
But within the dark cavernous longing
one dim light of acceptance can be seen.
It is bright,
loses its luster
and fades into a poignant star.
With the shallow rays it casts,
one can make their way out of the cavern.
It is there.

You just have to become accustomed to the dark.
It isn't fatal blindness.
It is temporary
and patience teaches us well.

Light the path to the sanctuary
and those struggling souls will come.
They will remove tattered robes of injustice
and crawl on plague-filled feet
to the opening of humanity.
Fall into this voice and swim.
It's always harder to hit a moving target.
Keep moving.
Tread water and with sure strokes
swim to the end of anxiety.

A lost little red wagon

I was looking for my toy.
It is red.
It is a really nice toy.
I've had since I was a little boy.
I played with it.
I brought it into my room
when I was going to go to sleep.

At night I could hear it whisper to me.
I would turn off the light
before she would enter.
I would ask her to leave
but the words never came.
It was only tears after the door
closed behind her.
It was only the feeling of disgust and revulsion.
My sex used as a tool for helping to cope with death.
Being the oldest I always did look like my father.

That is why I grew a beard,
so there was no mistake.
Instead I have a lost little red wagon.
It is gone
and all I've got to cover my face
are some hairs
and my tormented tears.

Boiled brew

Atop the world of forensic dealings,
I sting to unleash the code of desire in
my verbiage infested youth.
Holding scaffolding under my tiny nails,
I roast the utter useless
void of frustration reaping the
sounds of mice.

Chattering under the bright stars,
my teeth
under the sky of doom
slowly yellow
giving the ululating trips of
foraging through the final tampering of
leftist rigmarole.

Rolling massive joints of conceit,
I inhale the past.
It lingers like an unwanted odor
in some unclean men's room
in Paris.
The smell of urine stings my nostrils
and makes me leave in haste
forgetting to jiggle my member clean.

Swords of ivory covered steel
sting graceful curves
as it slices the beast of wires that
entangle all who've had the pleasure
of shock treatment.

They won't struggle with my forgotten mania
for it is well hidden and only
plays when it can win.

It is then that crusts of decay slide
into that forensic test
we all
watch fascinated
yet fear.
That lingering kiss
of death's sweat.

First time I read Poetry

It was in Syracuse, NY.
The bar was filled.
Open mike.
All styles welcomed.
Smoking was still allowed back then.
I twitched nervously
in my seat.
I remember going across
the border
and the guard asking

What is your purpose of your visit?

To read poetry. I answered

There was a pause.
And he let me in.

My name was called.
Heart thumping.
Read two heavy poems
about death.
There was supportive applause
and then at the end of the night
I got an invite to read in NYC.

Try that first brittle step.
A good gravel road
needs many stones.

Taking stock in suicide

Cleaning, cleaning, cleaning.
Those magical words.
The dead leave their
dust on old calendars.
Flipping the pages
gives you hives.

They've marked
little anniversaries
like the first time
you had a hard stool
or sat up on your own.
I write and yell
until I'm hoarse,
it's the only way
to silence me.

As a child
I found music class
to be limiting.
The drum gave me
a tribal edge to this
side of sanity.

Suicide
can cork the crap
out of your life.
Quit that wrist slitting,
gun shooting,
car inhaling,
bridge jumping
pill popping
masquerade
and hold onto today.

For there is nothing
more unappealing
than a drunk man
pissing
on his shoes.

Ontario

It is a land of loons, lakes
V-formations.
100 km/h speed limits
hockey on ponds
Niagara Falls fun-houses
starry nights
wood smoke out of rural houses
deer, moose and beaver
and the eternal joy
of watching those blessed trees
turn color
again.

Another leaving

Trailing through distant memories,
my mind remembers one
that jags a tiger smile.

Whenever a person leaves
the shelter,
be it a home,
comfy hotel room
or naval base;
a sense of loss occurs
that is far greater
than any rejection.
It is a sure sign of
moving on,
leaving tear stained glasses,
towels still unwrapped,
and the urge to float
in a TV numbing void.
Instead you are left
stranded;
on a platform terminal
or shady beach,
to remember the long sought
after peace.

A constant reminder
of how shallow
a person's armor truly can be.
How vague our mistrust
or how vain our loyalty.

In a shelter,
images are fully masked,
sometimes duly entertained
for we give puppet shows
twice a week,
and a striptease
on Saturday.
A breeze recovers our senses
as we sip another cup of coffee,
thinking of those days
before death, sorrow
and maintained sadness.

After a visit that was too long

It's not the friendly good morning smile
or the fact that the kids had a built-in sitter.
It's not the tears of homesickness
and the rows of pharmaceutical aides.
It's not the Coke cans that are consumed
or the beastly phone bill to your lover.
It's not the fact that your ex is coming over for a visit.

From the Alps to an isolated Canadian lake;
that's pretty far if it doesn't work out.
It doesn't and the palms on my hands
glisten with moisture,
awaiting the time in my life
when I will finally have the courage
to say no.

A trembling phone

Across the vast hallways of a ward,
sits the hollow sound of oxygen tanks singing.
I can hear the crisp clock click of inhalation.
It is an immediate release and ease
that can come from withdrawal.

Bandaged children cry in the dark,
fearing that sight and sound have been lost.
I have seen this ward full of its unwanted.
It is a row of cases that society
just doesn't want to see.
The overgrown tumor as large as a basketball
growing outside of his neck.
Cast of bodies neatly laying in a row.
The doctor doesn't come often.
He tires easily of the incurable.
It hurts his feelings and statistics.
It isn't good for business to say the words;
I just don't know...

But this is the voice we have.
A voice in the dark calling for a mother long dead;
a father out on the street.
This is the house of the unexplored.
A vainglorious calling
in the petty and stringent breaths of death.
The click of that oxygen mask
that sounds like a phone
being entombed.

Returning to that hospital

Some of you
might not know what it's like,
to have kooks
living under your roof.
It's about as arousing
as watching some 95 year old
wench strip.

I ask for my grandmother's help
and all I received
was a little bottle
of Tia Maria
placed on the kitchen table
to remind me of that last
swaggering suck.
It was four and half years ago.
It's easy to be a drunk,
folding oneself in half at neon bars,
holding up the counters
with over-priced booze.
I try to dampen any effect
on my neurons
as they hold together
some sense of sanity
in an ever increasingly
violent scene.

I roll one or two envelopes together
and steam them open
to see the truth.
So much,
for the unreal sensuous pouring
of mixed mint drinks.
I reach for water

and hold it tight
by my side.
I don't show my cards.
There seems to be reason
to these recurring nightmares.
Fondling
of an obscure nature.
My mother,
saw my brother and I
as semi-hairy children.
Fuck the inertia
that we had to fake.
Orgasms
can be fibbed by men
just as much as women.
It takes another minor
in superior acting.

She returned again
on Monday night,
with frock in hands
and asked coyly
if she could get under the cover.

You look so much like your father.

That's why I have a beard.
so there is no mistake.

She brushes my hair
and I kindly ask her
to leave.

What is it with molested men
and raped women?
The paws

of this infantile universe
should be severed
at the wrist.
We can then watch
with fascinated agony,
while it writhes in some
primordial pain.
This won't solve
the existence of these problems,
but it certainly will
hold the level
of striking thresholds steady.
Who's on trial;
the touched and ripped
or that panting pursuer?

Blood

I remember we were 18
and that darned condom broke.
We had been careful
but being young and not so practiced
it just broke
and I can't tell you how relieved
we both were
when her blood came.
I almost double bagged it
after that.
Well almost…

Rotten dates

Cursed by the adjacent stare,
I feel compelled to roam
ancient sites.
I would always fall asleep
in history class.
Now and again
that pre-historic yawn
gives me a start
and I look
for the nearest bench.

I know
that the detailed life
of a poet
is bleak.
I know
that the battle
of seduction
is won
dancing on splintered
opiate bottles.
I know
the fresh smell of Spring
brings rain and anxiety.
The sun needs to sequester
it's pure fabled juice
into a marketable string
of infomercials.

In jumping
between the living and dying,
I rummage in musty cupboards
finding forgotten Easter eggs.
I'm reminded of my past

when hands raise
and children flinch.
I recall the phrase my sanity
has tried to whisper,
' *Never trust a man*
who sells rotten dates.'

Purse on the counter

At the post office today,
a lady came in;
laid down her purse.

A vibrating noise
came from the bag.
She looked at me
with mischievous eyes
and hinted that same sound
really comes
from the subtle drawer
by the bed.

In the face of death

We don't know if we will scream
or if the cloud of hope
will gently carry us across the abyss.
We don't know if it will come in a parking garage
doing as mundane a task as parking a car.
It might come from choking on a carrot
or a piece of bread that it is too large.
It might come in an airplane crash
and your whole family will have to grieve
in the public light.
It might come when swimming
or in a distant gun shot gone astray
or in the fables of night
when nightmare and reality become one.

We don't know how it will be.
Sure there are astrologers that can predict.
But we can still change our way.
Path is not cast,
not beyond next hour or minute.

We don't know what will happen.
If it will be on a ward filled with a new plague
or in a back alley with a needle sticking in your arm.
It might come from a police club
with someone who mistakes you for somebody else.
It could happen.
Or die in a shallow grave in some field.

But whatever comes,
hold your inherent thoughts silent
for it does come.
There is no stopping it.
Release and place destiny
in the palms of acceptance.

Screaming flashbulb

Startling a vagrant owl
glaring into the woods.
A flashbulb goes off
to illuminate the brush.
Small do not cross tape
straddles the surrounding trees.
One step forward
toward the encircled finality.

Nubile chants in Spring

Cradle of fear
returned early this morning.
I've wandered around
the many cities of this world.
Whenever I feel
downtrodden or hurt,
I just roam the boulevards,
streets and lanes searching
for a parent who doesn't exist.

After my father died,
I would search in crowded malls
for his face,
sometimes almost seeing him
as I passed some middle-aged man
on the escalator.
I don't search as much as I used to
but will sometimes pick out
different characteristics
that sends a reminder.
I share these with my lover.
She is an epitome of strength,
many tears swell up in my eyes,
when I think of our coupling.
We had a hard path
and it has become easier
for understanding is at the core.

Fidelity is a word
that many seek
but most
only get a glimpse.
I love the star that shines
on her breast.

I love the birds in early morning
gathering strength for the day.
I love the floating feeling
of a plane taxiing onto a run way.
I am due for another round
of traveling.

Let's see what these
wild and dusty streets
hide.

Learning to bike

Mr. Melanson lived next door.
He was my little league coach.
He would cuss at us if
we played poorly.
We learned lots of new words
not to use in school.

That day I'd been trying
to ride my two wheeler.
The one with green and white tassles
and a green frame.
I would take an old tire
and help myself up
but couldn't quite do it.

Mr. Melanson came out
of his garage and grunted
Here
and grabbed hold of my bike seat.
Peddle
I started to peddle
and urged me to go *faster, faster, faster*
and before I knew it
he had let go
and I was riding down the street
passed the soon to be divorced
or dead
and letting my hair
blow wild.

Seeing undeniable patterns

Frothing,
as my father did in ancestral rage,
I tried to con my way
out of his induced madness.
Brother having periodic brain checks,
rounds of penicillin,
the trial of not once saying grace
with meaning.

Curdled memories flow swiftly
obstructing the view
my lover and I are trying to create.
We don't need no stinking
marriage certificate
to solidify our bond.
We don't crave the past
as a reminder
of our existence.
We just hold each other
on a cold Sicilian night
hoping
almost praying
for that created stain
to disappear from our
disjointed peripheral vision.

Tears

I cried for Lennon.
I cried for Reagan.
I cried for the Pope
but I never cried
when I got hit.

Riding the avenged

I wipe the nightmare
off my boiled skin.
Friends,
met on long journeys,
relayed anxious tones.
I listened
to their longing.
I searched
a Floridian beach
to try and scope
darkening memories.

I forge the relentless blooming
of a Scandinavian spring.
I create the devil's spear;
sharpened,
aimed
thrust through used car dealer's
coke filled chest.
I remove Band-Aids
on sallow children,
pleading for scraps of coal.
I crave the daily scourge
of confined incestual healing
as refrained notes
of baroque music
are played.
I strive to understand
the burned forests of Zingaro.
Coming up short,
only seeing scars.

I coax angels
to sing out of tune
for they also need humor
among trailing mourners.
I reveal steps of insanity
as toads migrate
across the road.
I relentlessly try to resolve
inner conflict
by trading
the unbecoming figures
that loom in stray shadows.
I cream the morning
and crave fated sleep.

In ancient storytelling,
the old taler
would always
be the first to yawn.

I am a bicycle seat

I love when she rides me
to work.
She straps on her multi-colored
helmet.
Firmly steps on the peddle and
zooms out into the dodging traffic.
I pass antique stores,
boarded up bars
and a drugstore that is open 24 hours.
She settles into me.
I'm holding up her frame.
She is trusting me fully.

Slamming on the brakes
to avoid a car.
She leaves my safety
for an instant
and then returns
to my reciprocating
warmth.

An abject call

The receiver was well lubricated
with indignation and quiet resolution.
It is easier to destroy with a flagrant tongue
then a felt-tipped whip.
I used to forgive the unseeing.
I could cope with their blindness.
Face lies and destructive deceit.
I could live in a shelter of absolution and constant pestilence.
I could acquire the appropriate terms
for repeat offences and related expenditures.
I could see that the retracting gums
would reveal the stinging pain of aging.
It begins with knuckles crunching under pressure.
A knee is constantly in flux awaiting a crack behind the
wheel.
It comes in the form of windless days
and the uneasiness from self-assured dignity.

I used to console myself that our sarcophagi of today
receive a bonus and ties on almost forgotten Father's Day.
Unless I'm mistaken,
I used to believe in truth.
In the unutterable cries of injustice
and the leggy trials of betrayal.
Now I refrain from the heart fluctuations.
Blood pressure constantly surveyed
as the stream of decisions are released
in the form of a 2:00 am cough.

I once knew the word stability.
It would always come in the form
of a shadowy violence.
It was tubular and never repented.

Only in a Toronto suburb after a fit of mania
and a file for divorce
did the stringent base fear subside.
I could honestly crush the words;
"*I am not afraid of you.*"
It took a few mind rotting months.
It took a couple of gluttonous years of egotistical annoyance.
Many a cigarette and bottle of wine
to accept the fate of life.
It remains in our beleaguered and bewildered souls
until the lock of transparency is shifted.
Our need for an insatiable tremor exists.

Believing can crush any oppressive suffering.
Believing will contain the necessary maps.
Believing is the battle-fed victor
in our dormant strength and chapped resolution.

Big Red Truck

You know that this truck
can haul lots of things
a dog
a lot of wood
a girlfriend
and your buckled child
eager to see the world
through the
window.

Tater dogs

Too many of these
and those wonderful arteries
in your chest
might need the help
of a paddle,
when you're 51.

Above the inescapable

Rush of feet pounding out beats.
Silver cars from beyond
all in a row
waiting.

In this trans-gendered city of instant repression
lights of another shade dimly appear.
Clocks have all stopped.
Only the cat purrs beneath her perch.
Grandma's bird has been eaten in gluttony and approbation.
It is a tremendous vague diet.
Distinct meaning is remembered.
It is found in an old encyclopedia
with the small picture of a Cyclops.
And we thought they were fables.
Close eyes of existence and patterns form
beneath navy lids.
Carnage and fruitful lust
doled out in heaps as large as mashed potatoes
and corn.
With regrettable silence,
chewing absolves terror.
A swallow of dissolving pills
as clerks chatter of office parties
and lurid affairs.

Oh, to sit at a copy maker
and rotate the Seeing Eye over my hand.
A resemblance acute;
yet infantile,
ashen from those canisters.

Unduly seen,
one can diffuse the extremities
and see the painted signal of warnings
in the shaded hues
of black and white.

Scented bath salts

I've always wanted
to chew on those plastic balls
that seems to adorn bathrooms
of the elderly.
They look more inviting
than any sweet, Gummi bear
or licorice stick.

I've had a thing about
bathrooms for awhile now.
My mother put her
drowned taint on the décor.
I have begun to accept
larger bathrooms
and those that have
a space for showers
and playful nudity.

I remember that morning.
It was the naked shake of death
extolling its solemn presence.
I hear the sound of putting
one's back against the stream.
It is all enveloping.
Creating a plethora of taunting memories
that must be respected
but from a firm distance.

Just as those bath salts
cover the masked odor,
it's best not to place
them under your tongue.

Blacking out

It was early in the morning
and I heard snoring in the room
next door.
I was 12.
Mom was on the bed
snoring loudly,
snoring too loudly.
I opened the renovated bathroom
and I saw my father blacked out
on the floor.
He was naked.
Near mom was an empty bottle
and spilled pills.
I tried to waken her
and she wouldn't.
Shaking, shaking, shaking.
I then called Dad
and he came to and called 911.
I said someone is trying to kill mom.

It would be years later
as an adult
that those flashing lights
and the memories of my father
and the black out
would faintly
grudgingly
sadly,
subside.

An abscess morning

Jostling images bounce
between shard streaks
of old footage.
It is the final week of December.
A time to gather courage
in the dark stray nights.
A time to float on an optical haze
of trusted acts of sedition.
A time to fold the petals of understanding
into thin origami strips.

With a shunted color of pink blossoms,
the diary of yesteryear is misplaced.
Gathering thick layers of dust
it grows its own set of tales
adjacent to slight and brief vignettes
of non-fiction.

A poet's life is full of bloodshed,
sorrow and timeless hours of convalescence.
They live in a shadow of a 4:00 am moon.
They sculpt crafted poems
on peeling park benches.
Scribble on flimsy napkins
in a local café.
They pull over to jot a line
and melt when they see
their names in print.

A poet must know when to quit.
When to take leave of the so-called incantation
and produce a stream of pictures that connect unduly
to the past and suffering.

With a small glass of milk,
perched on a screen porch,
the rocking motion of a creaky chair
moves in time
to the sleepy cries
of a breast-fed child.

Thin breath of waiting

Your tiny hand moves inside the crib.
It moves as does a small inch worm.
I hold it gently.
You move towards the warm hand
and open your eyes.
Seeing it is your dad,
you close your eyes again.

Inside your calmness
to sleep without fits;
I wait for you.

A quiet reassurance

I left a letter on our pillow.
A gift for your caressing features
and for the nights of lonely lust.
I left a note on our bed;
a small tender note
only to be read by your eyes.
It was to comfort you in times of pain
and hold you in times of duress.

I started the letter with:
Dear
and ended it with
Love,
I won't tell you what I put in the letter.
You'll have to open it.
You'll have to see the handwriting,
mixed sentences
and floating emotions.

Just know that there is a certain reoccurrence
that appears when life is empty.
When it does
suffering ceases.

Calmly place the stoker of compassion
between the cords of listen to the music flow
and watch its true essence seep in remembrance.
A flower will not wilt if pressed.
A love will not vanish if lost.
A lust will not dampen in water.
It grows just as animals, plants
and people grow.
With the incumbent insurance that life
and all of its existence will be alright.

It will be.
Just as the letter will say.
It will.
I *know* it will.

She emailed asking for money

My kids' mouths are open for food
as if small swallows awaiting worms.
The request came to ask to pay
for her children's daycare.
This was the second time
in two months.

I work 3 jobs to pay bills
and even then it just doesn't
seem to stretch.
The hungry ones across the country
wanting love and acceptance;
wanting a reality.
I can't seem to fault
the request
but I do
and in the end
when one must think
of our family first
it is a crashing
no.

I want to be a poet, Daddy

It's easier to wash cars
at red lights.
Dig down deep for coal.
Clean up vomit at the local school.
Put make-up on a cadaver.
Find bodies after a flood.

You can skin fish in a fish factory
or empty septic tanks with a hose,
be a divorce court judge.
You want to be a poet, son?

Are you sure?

Drugs

I knew that the time had come
to let you go grandma.
That last nurse came in
and gave you more morphine
than needed.
It took the winged flame of pain
away
and I saw the last curled smile fade
when your face vanished
into whiteness.

Debt

It is the amassed numbers
of what we owe.
This poet and librarian
scrimping together to get by.
It is what it is.
The bank and its glorious
interest-laden teeth,
and the small poems
and children's books
waiting to be repossessed.

for Emma

Your hand clenched in a droning fist.
Your body fights the faintly inevitable.
14 hours of surgery to reveal scars of suffering and want.

You can't write about the time you would first ride a horse
or visit Disney World.
You won't be able to laugh at the latest movie.
You won't be able to see the Pyramids, Taj Mahal
or Niagara Falls.
Your eyes will never see another star or half-moon.
They won't patrol the days searching for meaning.
They won't choose courses that are ill-suited;
plagued with being #1
or wallow in a crust of guilt.

Your face was without fear.
It looked up through the operating haze and
was allowed a chance to see beyond the shadows.
From within the darkness we come
and into the pale darkness you have gone.
You provided in your crushing shell;
a stem of beatific hope,
a starlit halo.

With a lighthouse uneasy flash;
you came.
With a storm of resistance;
you left,
leaving us but briefly
with each somnambulant turn;
to see your reflection
in our frightened eyes.

Garage sale

When she was young.
there was a small doll
that she held so close.
Now in her teens
that closeness is pushed away.
It lies on the grassed lawn
beside old lamp shades,
tattered comics
and that well loved doll.

She's lost an arm over the years
and has only one eye
but I can still see you dragging it
around the house.
Your friend, your protector.

Where is she, Daddy?
She needs to sleep too.

Now at the curb
she is placed in the box
that is marked 25 cents.
Selling treasure;
a bargain on that
fine trimmed lawn.

Family

Today,
walked through the empty house
they are at practice and band.

Today,
the cat meowed to be let out.
I did.
Now done.
One wisp of sweet grass incense
floats around the room.

Today,
I look at the photos on the piano.
Family in poses and laughter
and a strike towards goal.
Sometimes it takes
a quiet moment
to truly realize
the beauty of something
that's not there.

He called and I said good-bye

For years that phone has
been ringing.
Over and over again
and then the dreaded

Will you accept the charge.

Yes.

He asks for money.
A lot this time and I know
where it is going.
I know why it is there.
It is his veins that are hungry
and the pain pushes back
to blackness.
I can't anymore.
I won't.
He says

Fuck you

and

I'll kill you

and that might very well be
the last words I hear
from his chapped
and distant lips.

Practice, practice, practice

I've been driving my young one
to soccer for years.
They like his left foot.
They like his attitude.
On Monday,
being down by a goal he scored
3 in a row and they won 4 – 3.
Afterwards,
teammates jumped on him
and said you won the game for us.
He responded.
We all did as a team.

You don't find that in many 11 year olds.
It's been a challenging year this year.
He switched schools to learn French
and they don't like the outsider,
the seer
the gifted one.
They've historically tried to push down
those on top.

In the Fall he ran for Mayor of the school
and won.
He came home and said that many
of the kids were teasing him.
Being a Councilman myself
I said it is lonely at the top.

You do the best you can
in the short time you have here.
You have a gift and you must find
a way to use it.
His strong left foot

his beating heart
and his courage to try new things
has converted this 41 year old man
and the gray has come
but the sunset variant of life
is as beautiful as a sunrise
in overcast LA.

Coaching again

On Sunday night,
I was back on the field.
Giving encouragement, extending praise
to the youngsters in our community.
This is all about learning who we are.
Working together as a team
and finding the right moment
to put that elusive rolling ball
into the back
of the brand new net.

A jewel in the forest

My wife bought me a folly.
It is a statue.
6 feet high,
on a pedestal
over-looking the lake.
The lady is in a scantily clad robe
and her behind is luscious.

The kids asked me;
Where do you want to be buried?

I said tenderly,
out in the forest
behind her blessed bottom
and the sunset
going down
through
the pine needle
trees.

Who are you?

I look into the mirror
and see the shards in my veins.
I look into the mirror
and see my mom gently rocking
back and forth and that hospital
gown.

I look into the mirror
and ask why am I rushing life?
Let it take its course.
SS troops and the Nazis
can wait.
There'll be time enough
after tea.

I look into the mirror
and wonder how as an 11 year old,
I coped with seeing Anne's bedroom
in Amsterdam.
Yet I still had a capacity to
laugh on the bed.

I look into the mirror
realize that with all of those
deaths, something good must come
and it did
in the transformation of our two kids.
The love in me is so great
that I'll almost break.
When given the choice
the little one said take me
so you can save two.

I look into the mirror
and wonder how heavy
a divorce is and does it weigh as
much as being a pall-bearer
at a friend's funeral.

I look into the mirror
and I see her undressing.
I know I shouldn't paw
but it can't be helped
when you are as beautiful
as the moon.

I look into the mirror
and that it can be done
gathering votes to represent
and then turning gray with worry.

I look into the mirror
and realize that life is full
of blemishes,
a couple of scratches
and the scab bleeds,
so it's best to leave it alone.

I look into the mirror
and love holding the hands of
people who need warmth
for the house can be as cold
as a heart.

I look into a mirror
watch the whiskers fall into
the sink and await complaints
from stopping up the drain.

I look into the mirror
and can see the future
reflecting back and all that
is needed is to laugh
with kids before noon
and night.

I look into the mirror
and can see my teeth falling out,
the gaps between truths widening
and now focusing on the next bloom.

I look into the mirror
and the sanctity of being loved
is being realized.
I kiss those lips goodnight
and moisten the afternoon with release.

I look into the mirror
and see that you can never
assume.
I look into the mirror
and see the children curled
under each arm,
a book resting on my rising chest.

I look into the mirror
and see that you've never
left,
best to just get out another chair
there's always room for one more.

I look into the mirror
and wince, cock-eyed and yodel
like Tarzan would baying at the moon.
I look into the mirror
and the mirror always holds still
for me.

About the Author

Photo courtesy of John Maurice

T. Anders Carson has had his poems published in 37 countries including translations into French, Greek, Japanese and Swedish. He is a Helene Wurlitzer Foundation Fellow. He is a full member of the League of Canadian Poets. He has read his work from Los Angeles to London including stops in Cairo, Paris, Stockholm and Swansea. He opened up for The Magnetic Fields in Oslo, Norway. He currently resides on the outskirts of a rural village in Ontario, Canada. He lives with his wife, two kids and two cats. He can be seen moving motions as a Councilman, dealing mail and selling stamps as a Postmaster for Canada Post, teaching classes of poetry and passing soccer balls on a field.

·

Made in the USA
Charleston, SC
10 May 2013